7 HABITS
OF
HIGHLY
HAPPY
PEOPLE

7 HABITS *of* HIGHLY HAPPY PEOPLE

BIX BENDER

GIBBS · SMITH
PUBLISHER

SALT LAKE CITY

99 98 97 96   10 9 8 7 6 5 4 3 2 1
Text copyright © 1996 by Bix Bender

This is a Peregrine Smith Book, published by
Gibbs Smith, Publisher
P.O. Box 667
Layton, Utah 84041

Design by J. Scott Knudsen, Park City, Utah
Printed and bound in the U.S.A.

Library of Congress Cataloging-in-Publication Data
Bender, Bix, 1949–
Seven habits of highly happy people / Bix Bender.
p.   cm.
ISBN 0-87905-731-9
1. Happiness. I. Title.
BF575.H27B45   1996
158'.1—dc20   95-42292
                                     CIP

To Madge, the unsung,
indispensable hero
of all my books, and
to Sally, who makes
me happy.

Acknowledgments

This book would not have been possible without the kind and generous help of dozens of people who took the time to tell me their happy habits. All of you know who you are. Please also know that I thank you very much.

Contents

Happiness makes up in height what it lacks in length.
Robert Frost

When I was a young man and leaving my southern home for the first time to take a summer job in California, I got lots of advice on how to be happy and how not to get homesick. My Aunt Julie told me if I ever felt down to just imagine how much worse things would be if I were in hell. Her husband, Uncle Frank, added, "Of course, if you're planning on going there, thinking about it won't cheer you up much."

My cousin Wayne told me a girlfriend was the best way to keep from getting depressed and the best way to meet a girl was to strike up a conversation by saying, "Lovely weather we're having, isn't it?" He further assured me this line would always be appropriate where I was going, as it never rained in California. I arrived in California in the midst of a year-long drought. It never rained, but if I'd said "Lovely weather we're having, isn't it?" to anyone, I would have been told to go to hell.

So, I shelved Wayne's advice. Aunt Julie's too—not because I was planning on going there, but because I was certain that imagining such a hopeless place would only increase my depression.

The advice I did take came from my father and mother. Dad, as he said good-bye with a smile and a firm handshake that included a warm clasp on my back, advised me, "Remember, the only way to get a smile is to give one." Mom hugged me too and said, "And also remember, no one smiles back at a boy who's wearing dirty underwear." How could anybody tell if I had clean underwear on or not, I asked her. "People know these things," she replied. That kind of motherly logic is hard to argue with.

Is happiness as simple as clean underwear and a smile? Not necessarily by themselves, but they are habits that create a happy feeling. And happy feelings energize and increase happiness exponentially. If something makes you feel good, other things feel better. One laugh almost always leads to another. Comedians know this. Once they break the ice and get a good laugh out of you with their A material, they refer back to it again and again and get you to laugh at almost anything they say. Once you start laughing, it feels so good you just want to keep doing it. Having one or more happy habits can do the same thing—put you on the path to happiness.

Why are some of us happy and others not? What is it that makes someone a happy person? A million dollars? A big house? A day without a phone call from a telemarketer? A date on Saturday night? A morning to sleep in? A perfect cup of coffee? For some of us, one or more of these would make us happy; for others, it would be something else. But the secret to having a happy life is not to be constantly laughing, but to be able to bounce back from a bout with unhappiness, to use little tricks—some happy habits—to jump-start our minds and revitalize our energy.

This book does not contain a single scientific solution to unhappiness. No psychiatrists or psychologists were involved in its writing. To get material for this book, I wrote letters to everyone I know and everyone they knew and then some. The letter asked, "What are your happy habits? What do you do to turn away the blues?" One thing led to another and the responses poured in from all over the country. I edited, paraphrased, and signed up some of the respondees for the witness protection program. Then I added advice received in conversation. These ideas, along with some of my own, became the 7 *Habits of Highly Happy People.*

I am happier because of what I have learned in writing this book. I believe you will be happier from reading it.

Twenty years ago on the road to Globe, Arizona, I met a man named Joe, a Chiricahua Apache. I never knew his last name, nor he mine. But I have never forgotten what he said:

Being happy is a feeling every living creature can have. For corn it is water, sun, and room to grow. For the coyote it is a full belly, fresh water, and room to roam. For me it is the feeling that tomorrow will be a good day. And I will not go to bed without convincing myself of this.

Spirit
Dusting

As we go through life we're constantly being rained on by cosmic dust. It comes from out there—space. Then there's the dust our own world generates. It comes from everywhere. Our spirits accumulate dust of a different sort: little slights and disappointments, hurtful things that are said to us or that we say to someone else; heartaches that heal but leave a residue of mistrust; dreams that crash and burn but leave a fine ash of hopelessness.

To make room for happiness, our spirits need a regular dusting. When you stir this dust up, you may cry a little, hurt a little, and whine a while. That's okay, venting anger is how you get rid of it. You can't do a good dusting without getting some of it in your eyes. Let the tears wash the dust away. Kiss it good-bye. Then embrace your clean spirit and get on with your life.

My roommate and I stay happy by making sure we've got one night a month to be unhappy. We plan on it. We wallow in it. We love it. We rent a heartbreaking old movie, we read aloud heartbreaking passages from Harlequin Romances, we eat brokenhearted burgers and lovesick french fries, and we tell each other all the rotten things men have done to us. Talk about cathartic! Talk about pathetic! Talk about fun!

Paulette D., Graphic Artist
Denver, Colorado

I have a dartboard that keeps me happy. When somebody crosses me, their picture goes on it. If I don't have a picture of whoever made the mistake of making me mad or upset, I draw one. I'm a lousy artist, so that makes it even better because they look like hell. I have seven darts. Each one has a name. There's "You talking to me?" "Cross me, will ya!" "Is that right, Mister Know It All?" "Oh, yeah?" "Take that!" "What did you say?" and "Eat worms and die!"

Lorena H., Medical Technician
Los Angeles, California

I make up songs. I can sing my own songs that embarrass, condemn, or humiliate anyone who has embarrassed, condemned, humiliated me. They might not be good songs, but it works. Every time.

Stuart W., Songwriter
Fort Worth, Texas

Blues today? Okay. But not tomorrow!
A simple formula, but that's my plan for dealing with depression. If I've had the butt of my soul kicked around all day, I will not let it be that way tomorrow. If today growled and snarled and chewed on me, okay. But tomorrow I bite back.

Doris W., Surveyor
Seattle, Washington

When I've got a fight going with depression, loneliness, or the blues, I have two ways to deal with it.

The first one is to rev up my ol' Sears lawn tractor that's a good twenty years old, put some nice music in my ears, and spend the next five to seven hours mowing and beautifying my two acres. Just the feeling of accomplishing something helps a lot.

The second way is to have an Aunt Dorothy. Someone you can depend on to listen, to care, and to help you see the bright side and give you hope. Everyone needs an Aunt Dorothy, and we all need to be Aunt Dorothys to someone else who is in distress.

Bobbie Jo O., Businesswoman
Knoxville, Tennessee

I've got somebody I call whenever I get down. My brother. He listens, I bitch and whine. When I'm winding down with my moaning—so far he's hardly said five words, I guess—he somehow turns the conversation to the Cleveland Indians. Doesn't matter if it's baseball season or not, we're fanatics. So we spend another twenty minutes figuring out what's right or wrong with "the tribe" and reliving great games of the past; then we say good-bye and I don't feel down anymore. Matter of fact, I feel pretty okay.

**Jason B., Carpenter
Cleveland, Ohio**

Whenever I'm feeling like the world's grand all-time loser, that's when I say to myself, "All right, so I've dropped the ball a time or two. Who hasn't?" Then I say to myself, "Lots of people have, that's who! In fact, everybody! Nobody's perfect and I'll prove it to you!" Then I go to a file I keep on the *Great Screw-ups of the Rich and Famous.* It's crammed with magazine and newspaper articles I've clipped and notes I've made from books I've read about the great mistakes of the high and mighty and even the holy.

After I read a few of these over, I realize whatever I messed up or missed out on is not nearly as bad as what somebody else who's a lot better off than me has done.

Pat B., Florist
Santa Barbara, California

I look at it like this; the bad things that come your way you just got to get over. It's the good things that come your way you have to know how to deal with.

I'll give you an example: I got a friend who went to Atlantic City and hit the slots for right around $80,000 after taxes. Of, course this made him happy. And, of course, this also made his wife and kids happy. All this happiness lasted about 24 hours. That's when they all started arguing about how to spend the money. The wife wanted to save it all, the kids wanted new cars, my friend wanted a boat.

He comes to me, has a Hudy and a shot and asks for my advice. I says the only thing you can do is split it up and give everybody their share. You're a family. It's their money as much as yours. If one of them had won it, wouldn't you have felt like you deserved a little something? It's just like your paycheck, buddy. You don't get all of that, do you?

So, 'cause what I say makes good sense, he takes my advice. He gives his wife $20,000 and she invests it in a mutual fund. He tells his two kids to save their money and buy their own cars, but he puts twenty grand for each one in a trust fund. It's theirs if they want to go to college. If they don't, they get it when they turn twenty-five. Then he takes the last $20,000 and buys his boat. It wasn't as big as he wanted, but it was better than nothing.

That's how I try to keep it on the road. The bad things, I shrug them off. The good things, I put a lot of thought into.

Ron K., Bartender
Cincinnati, Ohio

I figured out a long time ago the way to be happy is to be willing to deal.

When bad times come along, I don't want them—but that's life. Sometimes things go real wrong. But I don't think it's the devil coming after me or that God is mad at me. I just think that's life, and if I am alive—which I am and that's a fact I always take comfort in—then I firmly believe I have the God-given ability somewhere within me to deal with whatever comes along. Sometimes I've got to reach deep down way past the pain and sorrow, but somewhere inside me is the strength I need to work through whatever it is that's troubling me. The key, and I believe it's also the secret of happiness, is to not give up. To keep dealing with it until sooner or later I start to see some light coming through from the end of the tunnel, and that means good times are coming back again.

Jordan H., Farmer
RFD, Michigan

How I escape the blues depends on what kind of blues I've got. Here are some of the ways I lose some of the blues.

☛ Call my sister. We've both been through so much in the past few years. We can cry over the phone about everything; then we laugh about crying, and feel better.

☛ Call my old boyfriend. We're both married now, but we still make each other laugh. (Side note: We haven't seen each other in many years. He's just a wonderful friend.)

Jamie A., Television Producer
Fairview, Tennessee

When I get down it's like I get mad. I pick up a baseball bat and hit something with it over and over until I feel better. Hitting people is illegal and unrealistic, so I use a stack of pillows. Try it, it works. I've broken three bats over the years and had some good workouts to boot. (Kind of explains why I'm still single, though, doesn't it?)

Ginny W., Florist
Pittsburgh, Pennsylvania

To ward off the blues I have a good cry and really wallow in it.

Brooke A., Artist
Peagram, Tennessee

I keep a drawer, a big deep drawer, where I put all the junk and clutter that comes into my life that I don't know what to do with: Pieces of things that I've forgotten what they're for, gag gifts people have given me, all the little geegaws and doodads that come into my life that I have no real use for but can't bring myself to just throw away. When I get down in the dumps, I dump the contents of everything in this drawer into a cardboard box. I then mail it to a friend, one with a sense of humor. I enclose a note that says "take what you want, then add your own clutter to it and pass it along to someone else." Getting rid of this "little stuff" lifts my spirits just as much as if I'd packed up some actual troubles and sent them away.

**Nana W., Resource and Development Director
Portland, Oregon**

When I'm having a bad time and everybody is getting on my nerves, I do something really nuts. I grab somebody I feel like smacking in the face because of something stupid they just said or did, and I give 'em a great big hug. I do it without thinking; it's just a release mechanism I use. It always startles both the person I hug and myself as well. Sometimes they look at me like I'm crazy, but usually they give me an awkward little hug back. This usually leads to two whole new attitudes on this little planet.

Bruce H., Teacher
Houston, Texas

When I have a bad day I write a letter to the President. I tell him everything that's bothering me and ask him if he's ever had a day like mine. If I'm mad at my mother, I tell him. If I'm having money troubles, I tell him. If I'm hurt because of something my husband did or didn't do, I tell him. It's my right as an American to write my President. So, I do. He writes me back too. I've got a nice little drawer full of form letters telling me he was happy to hear from me, he appreciates my taking the time to write him, and thanking me for telling him my feelings. (My friend Mary writes the Pope, but I'm not Catholic.)

Eunice C., Homemaker
St. Paul, Minnesota

keep a package of multicolored balloons in a drawer in my kitchen. When I come home at night, I make a list of all my troubles. I give each one a color. Red is for who or what is making me angry. Blue, of course, is for who or whatever is making me blue. Yellow is for whenever I have failed to stand up for myself. Green is, obviously, for something or someone I'm envious of. Orange is for the idiots in my life. Purple is reserved for special idiots, and black for special days. When I come home, I choose the appropriate balloons, blow them up really big to where they almost burst, and using a heavy Sharpie, I write on each balloon who or what they represent. If they're orange idiot balloons or purple special idiot balloons, I also draw faces on them and give them names—like Harry the Stupid Jerk, Belinda the Beast, Bob Bonehead, and Dorinda the Bimbo! Next, I put *Joan Jett's Greatest Hits* on the stereo and dance around with an antique hat pin that belonged to my wonderful and formidable Aunt Gertie, and pop them one by one. I then hunt up my family, give them big hugs, and together we dance around the kitchen and cook dinner. I never have the blues, but I do have a big balloon bill.

**Taylor R., Legal
Secretary
New York, New
York**

29

I don't give a whit for lamenting, losing, or mourning. I laugh, I scream, I yell. That's it. These are the best emotions for dealing with depression, frustration, or heartache. You can't cope if you suck it in and let it dribble out in tears. Scream bloody murder! Laugh your head off! Tell the world about it! Now you're talking! Let the wimps, the whiners, and the whipped wear it out. As for me, I let it out!

Barney H., Merchant Marine
Portland, Oregon

I look at it this way: When I'm not happy it's because I'm internally disagreeing with what's going on in my life. So I take a walk by myself, talk to myself, and try to figure out what it is that I disagree with that's happening to me. It usually turns out that I'm expecting somebody else to be acting some other way than they are. Well, this is when I face the fact, time and time again, that I can change myself but not somebody else. So I have a choice: I can accept them or reject them. What I do is my decision. Once I make it, I'm in agreement with myself. And, that makes me happy.

Paul W., Salesman
Long Island, New York

S w e a t

I t

O u t

When asked at the beginning of baseball spring training one year what his cap size was, Yogi Berra replied, "I don't know. I'm not in shape yet."

Of course, hat size isn't affected by how buffed and toned a body is, but experts tell us that regular exercise has an impact on the well-being of our spirits. After all, the body is the temple of the soul, and a run-down temple is a pretty good sign that the spirit needs a little sprucing up too.

After a day of strenuous physical activity such as raking leaves or moving furniture or gardening, a lot of us will say we're tired—but it's a good tired and a happy tired. Certainly this good tired has to do with the fact that we got something done that needed doing, but it also means that our minds and bodies worked together in a pleasing way. The mind had the will to do the job and the body did it!

When you exercise, you're doing something for yourself—body, mind, and spirit. A lot of folks find this to be a very happy habit.

I keep a list of chores that should be done around the house. These are things that I never seem to have time for (or don't want to have time for) but need to be done. Things like touching up the wood trim with paint, reglazing a window, caulking the tub, etc. Not exactly fun ways to spend my time. Anyway, when I have a problem or I am bored, I select a project from this list and complete it. If I have a big problem to deal with, I usually finish more than one project before I quit. When I do stop, it's instant gratification time. The happy feeling I get from accomplishing something I have procrastinated clears my mind and usually helps me find a solution to my problem.

Andrew B., Booking Agent
Nashville, Tennessee

Aerobics, aerobics, aerobics. The lights, the music, the people, the exercise! Who could feel down with all that going on? I go five times a week for hour-long sessions. I look forward to it, I feel great doing it, and afterwards I feel healthier, sleep better, and I just stay in an overall good frame of mind because of it.

Gwen H., Registered Nurse
Chicago, Illinois

'**I**'ve got to get something done on my own when I get down, because feeling out of control is usually what gets me down. So, what I do is focus on finishing something, anything, then I do it. It may involve others, but I make the decisions and I get it done.

Carole D., Waitress
Dover, Delaware

As a mother of six children, I find that the days of routine can sometimes really be a drag on my spirits. I've found a good, brisk walk in the quieter hours of the morning really helps set my day off on the right course. It freshens the routines to come and heightens the enjoyment of the unexpected events that occasionally happen.

If the weather's right, I also like to spend a few peaceful moments in the middle of our hammock in the middle of the afternoon. And there's nothing like getting down on the ground and playing with a toddler. Those are the best smiles and laughs you can be around. Totally contagious.

Ellison G., Homemaker
Layton, Utah

I can deal with any problem if my house is clean and I don't have to clean it.

I remember sitting in a business meeting and suddenly blurting out, "Maybe I should just get the fire department to come to my house, turn on the hoses, and clean it out!"

No one noticed. They were probably worrying about how messy their houses were too. But this made me realize just how important a clean, neat home was to my happiness. The problem is, I never feel like I have the time to clean my house. I have so many other obligations. Then it dawned on me: obligation is the key to getting things done. I found seven other friends who were having the same problem I was, and we drew up a solemn pact to clean each other's houses. We formed the "I Hate Cleaning Mine, But I'll Clean Yours Club!" Every Thursday we are all obligated to clean somebody else's house. We each load up with cleaning supplies and head out to clean somebody else's house. We rotate from one member's

house to the next
one's. This sounds
crazy, I know, but it
makes us happy.

**Janet S., Bank Teller
Baltimore, Maryland**

I think how I plan my vacations is how I stay happy. I get three weeks a year.

Two of those weeks are always different, but one of those weeks is always the same. It's the one that's always the same that keeps me happy. This is the one I schedule each year for major housecleaning. Fifty-one weeks a year I do my best to keep my

40

job, raise my kids, love my husband, and in my spare time (ha!), keep my house clean. But you can't do the Big Clean in your spare time. So once a year I take a week off and clean, really clean, house. My husband takes a couple of days during that week to help with the heavy stuff. My kids are responsible for part of it too. But mostly it's me. After all, I'm the one it really matters to. Mike, my husband, thinks a dust bunny is a maid for Hugh Hefner. My kids think clean windows is a new computer program. I think a clean house is heaven. And, it's amazing how long a really clean house can stay that way . . . not a year, but long enough to relax and energize me to do it again next year.

April H., Stockbroker
Philadelphia, Pennsylvania

As the product of a classical education, my first impulse is to say, "nothing in excess" and "know thyself." Of course, my second impulse is to say, "sleep and liquor." But here are my standbys to fight the blues:

1. Aerobics followed by a little free-weight lifting. Who can be down when their pecs are pumped?

2. Polishing silver (inherited silver, that is). The ancestors who polished it in years past survived wars and depressions. So can I, so can you.

Thomas B., Antique Dealer
London, England

To ward off the blues, I take a long horseback ride in the woods.

Allen B., Training Supervisor
Baton Rouge, Louisiana

I consider myself lucky to be one of the world's happy people. Life's not always a picnic, but overall I give it a big thumbs up! My recipe for happiness is as follows:

Exercise. I do this often because being outdoors and using my body makes me happy. Of course, there's also some vanity involved in keeping fit. But that's okay, there's vanity involved in everything we do, from putting on makeup to picking out sunglasses. Best for me, though, is that exercise serves as preventive maintenance to avoid depression and to help me handle stress as well.

Take a walk. Going with a friend increases the happy quotient. But sometimes it's good to go alone so I can spend a little time with myself. If I'm feeling down, I go right ahead and wallow in my sorrows. I think a little sorry wallowing is good for you every now and then.

Yoga. I enjoy the physical exertion and the mental relaxation, but when I'm fighting off the blues, I pay particular attention to the words of instruction: "Be centered. Focus. Let go. Relax. Take a deep breath and image all your toxins and troubles being expelled when you let it out.

Lace up the roller blades, put on the Spandex and Lycra, and take off! I tell people that roller blading is as fun as it looks, and you've got to admit that it looks fun. If I'm out of energy and low at the end of the week, I have the Friday-night skates in San Francisco to look forward to. The Midnight Rollers meet on Fridays at 8:30 P.M. at the Ferry Building. From 150 to 300 people assemble to skate about thirteen miles around "The City." The scenery is magnificent, and whooping and hollering through the streets of San Francisco is a great release. At the end, you feel like you should get a T-shirt that says "I survived the Friday-night skate.

Martha W., Computer Consultant
Palo Alto, California

Deal
a Happy
Meal

Had a hard day? Feel like it's a rat race out there and you're the cheese?

When the going gets tough, some of us crave an immediate "fix" and run to the kitchen for comfort. And that's not all bad. A snack of carbohydrates, we're told, will boost our energy level and make us better able to cope. The problem is, there's not always a baked Idaho spud at the ready, so we grab whatever's convenient. Personally, I feel worse after hosting a pity party of salty chips and gooey brownies, but give me a mixed bag of raw ingredients and an hour in the kitchen or at the grill, and I'll cook my bad karma away.

Whatever satisfies your cravings, it's true that there is comfort in food. Choose carefully and keep some crunchy foods on hand—lots of chewing is an outlet for aggression. Open up the pantry, break out the pots and pans, and make yourself a recipe for happiness.

When I've had a bad day, or week, or whatever, I have a three-step program to happiness.

1) On the way home from work, I pick up Chinese food for everybody, including soup and some fresh grapes.

2) We eat supper on paper plates so there's very little cleanup.

3) I curl up on my bed with a good mystery and a bowl of fruit. I read and eat grapes and just let everything else on my mind drift away. When I get sleepy, I turn out the light and go to dreamland. Tomorrow is another day.

Maryann B., Insurance Saleswoman
Phoenix, Arizona

When things unexpectedly go wrong or depression jumps out without warning and nails me, I don't have any kind of plans. I just try to weather it out. But if I *know* a bad day is coming, I know exactly what to do to keep my spirits up through the longest of days. The day I'm expecting troubles I get up early enough to have a long, leisurely, hot, and filling breakfast—good food that sticks to my ribs. If I can have this small pleasure, then I can keep my head up and take what comes till the sun goes down and then some.

Stewart S., Truck Driver
Mobile, Alabama

To ward off the blues, I eat frozen yogurt.

Amanda Y., Clerk
Honolulu, Hawaii

What really makes me happy is a cold beer on a hot summer day after mowing my lawn.

James C., Writer
Worcester, Massachusetts

There's nothing like a plate of mashed potatoes with a little ranch dressing mixed in to boost my sagging spirit to zippity-doo-dah level.

Sandy Y., Hair Stylist
Sacramento, California

f I need a little comforting or cheering up, I love to
curl up under the covers of my bed with a crisp,
cold, red Delicious apple to chomp on.

Pam M., Massage Therapist
Belpre, Ohio

f I'm feeling low I make homemade bread. I pound
and knead that dough as though it were all my
problems. I pull it and push it into shape. Then, I bake
it and eat a couple of slices while it's still warm from
the oven. It tastes great and I feel good.

Kay R., Day-care Worker
Hartford, Connecticut

I don't get depressed too often, but when I feel depression coming on I head for the kitchen. I dump all my troubles in a mixing bowl, stir them up, roll them flat, cut them out, and bake them away. Then I eat them, although sometimes I give them to whoever is bugging me and let them eat the troubles they give me. I'm talking about baking cookies here. Sour Grape Cookies, Flat Broke Raisin Bars, Heartache Coconut Drops, Wooly Worm Macaroons, How Dare You Prune Filled Oatmeal Squares, Stop Picking On Me Snickerdoodles, and of course, What A Butthead You Are Brownies . . . or, depending on the person—sometimes including myself—Brown-nose Brownies.

Irlene V., Dietician
San Antonio, Texas

Sometimes if I'm feeling down, I'll call some friends and invite them to dinner that evening. This works in two ways to fight the blues: it forces me to keep busy preparing a meal better than they could have had at home, and I know I have to gear up to be a lively, gracious hostess for the evening, because nobody wants to come to my house for dinner and listen to me whine. If I get a compliment on one of the dishes I fix, that's an extra bonus.

**Theresa W., Communications
  Representative
Kansas City, Missouri**

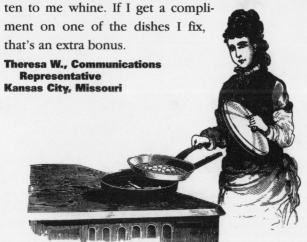

Happy
Heart
Kick
Starts

When your battery runs down and you find yourself glaring more than smiling, it's time for a power boost. Do something that brings a smile to your face and pleasure to your heart. Music soothes the savage beast and the gloomy one too, reading is relaxing, a nap gives the body a break and refreshes the mind, a little shopping spruces up the countenance, a hot bath steams away the blues, a trip to the garden cultivates a happy spirit. In other words, take a little time for yourself. It's a wonderful way to make a day happier.

When I feel particularly blue, I pamper myself with a couple of hours shopping. I don't go for clothes or pricey knickknacks—too expensive an indulgence, and I might feel worse the next day for having been extravagant. Instead, I buy some beautiful fresh flowers—maybe a plant perhaps a bouquet. Then I shop for a scented votive candle—not the common $.99 variety, but a lovely $1.49 kind with an exotic fragrance like hyacinth, lilac, black orchid, or lily of the valley. I take my treasures home and place them in the prettiest holders. Then I collect a book I've been saving or a new magazine, prop myself comfortably in a nest of fluffy pillows, and pretend my name is Asterbilt. I guess it's a form of aroma therapy, but it goes way beyond that for me. It's more like spending a few dollars and hours to feed my soul.

I don't know if this would work for men. Maybe they should buy a model car and put it together carefully with toothpicks. The glue would be their aroma therapy.

Marilyn T., Health Care Receptionist
Helena, Montana

I have a simple recipe for joy that will work for anyone still sane enough to know that Newt Gingrich is just a bad joke foisted on the American people by the ghost of Eugene McCarthy: eat pancakes, listen to a baseball game on the radio, and take a ride to somwhere you've never been.

Charlie B., Newsstand Manager
Memphis, Tennessee

When I'm in a funk:

☛ I read seed catalogs for hours on end, planning luscious cottage gardens.

☛ I spend a guilt-free day in bed reading all the magazines that have piled up, unread, for months.

☛ I ignore work and talk on the phone to my best friend for hours until the cordless goes dead.

☛ I walk through my yard looking at all my flowers.

☛ I paint something in my house a new shade of pink!

Lin B., Photographer
Greenbriar, Tennessee

When I feel bad, I fake feeling good. I've never found any satisfaction in letting myself wallow in despair or loneliness. If I feel unhappiness coming on, I force a smile on my face and I get right into doing something. Everybody thinks I'm happy, and pretty soon I am.

**Lindsay A., College Student
Atlanta, Georgia**

If it's been one of those dog-eat-dog days and I feel like I've been wearing Alpo underwear, I fill the tub with hot water, light candles all around, put on some soothing music, and give my psyche a good psoak.

Tracy B., Cosmetics Salesperson
Louisville, Kentucky

Go to a ball game; cheering cheers me up. Hot dogs and suds are part of the therapy too. (That's root beer suds, by the way.)

Josh M., Printer
Biloxi, Mississippi

When I get down, I pray and gamble. I pray for luck; then I go out and buy five lottery tickets. I play the same numbers every week and everybody I know knows the numbers I play and tells me I'm wasting my money. When I die, I want to be buried with a prayer book in one hand and a fist full of new lottery tickets in the other. If that's the week I hit it, there'll be a scramble to dig me up the likes of which haven't been seen since the days of the gold rush. I won't get the money, but I'll sure get a laugh out of it . . . Thinking about that makes me pretty happy right now.

Sonny T., Newspaper Deliveryman
Tampa, Florida

What do I do when I'm down? I hate to sound like a Pollyanna—but, actually, I seldom do feel blue. Don't you hate people like that?

It's probably in the genes, or chemistry, or whatever. Why is my sister Dot a natural worrier? My daughter Sheilagh a pessimist? Why are some people nonsmilers? If I could figure that out, I'd be rich (maybe like the Prozac people).

I asked my husband, George. He says he just forgets it—thinks of something else. (The macho thing, no doubt!)

But anyway, when I do occasionally feel low, here are some of the things I might do:

☛ Buy a bunch of flowers at the grocery store flower department.

☛ Get out of the house and do something, anything!

☛ Or conversely to the above, curl up by myself with a good book and a spirited old-fashioned cocktail.

Cecilia "Cissy" S., Housewife
Rockville, Maryland

Computer games are my escape to happiness. Sometimes I like to sit in front of a fifteen-inch screen and blow away anything that moves. It's only a game, but it's a real stress-buster.

Dave M., Musician
Nashville, Tennessee

I wash away the blues by standing in the shower until my head clears and the hot water runs out.

Michael A., Street Vendor
Albany, New York

Each week I write down the words to an inspirational song or poem on paper and tape it someplace where I'll see it every day. I use it to remind me how I want to live my life. This week, I have the lyrics to "Louie, Louie" taped to my bathroom mirror.

Nancy W., Public Relations
Nashville, Tennessee

Blow off an afternoon and go to the movies.

Ron M., Salesman
New York, New York

If I need cheering up, I dye my hair a different color. It all started when I had a friend who, when depressed, would have a different body part pierced. Well, I have enough holes in my head as it is, so I opted for hair coloring. It's less painful, less permanent, and more fun.

Barrie J., Actress/Electrician
Los Angeles, California

I beat the blues by heading for the nearest children's playground where I swing on the swings as high and fast as I can. I enjoy the near-flying sensation. I am exhilarated by the sense of freedom. And the carefree childhood feelings I carry away with me after one of these sessions gives me a big boost when I go back to dealing with the big kids in the big world outside the playground.

Anna N., Advertising Copywriter
Buffalo, New York

66

Well, I keep pretty busy doing what I like, and that keeps me pretty happy. But every now and then, after a hard day or two and I need a little boost to the ol' spirits, I like to plug an old Gene Autry or Roy Rogers movie into the VCR, stretch out on the couch with my wife beside me, and take a little trip into an old-timey place where there was straight shootin', straight talkin', and straight-ahead livin'. Nothing went wrong that couldn't be put right by an honest man and a good cowboy song or two.

Duane H., Rancher
Because, Texas

I shake off the blues by turning up my stereo very loud and singing along at the top of my lungs. This works best in my car; at my apartment it can lead to embarrassing calls from my neighbors. I usually duet with Pat Benatar or Mick Jagger, though lately I've found Brooks and Dunn to be decent accompanists.

Loretta W., Construction Worker
Detroit, Michigan

When I start to feel a little sad for no particular reason, I curl up with a small notebook of poems that I have collected over the years. Some are sad, some are happy, some are funny, some are inspirational, some are just silly. I flip through my little book and read the ones that appeal to my mood. The further I get into my book, the further the sadness is pushed away. Soon, instead of feeling sad for no particular reason, I'm feeling happy for a lot of reasons.

Dorothy A., Retired Secretary
Knoxville, Tennessee

When I get the blues, I hit the sidewalk and walk. But I don't walk in a normal manner. I walk like John Cleese did in the Monty Python skit where he played the Minister of Silly Walks. It's sort of a knees out, arms akimbo, heel-toe, very silly walk. You can't do it and not laugh. Of course, I get laughed at as well, but it takes my mind off my troubles.

Michael C., Tour Guide
San Francisco, California

I dump my troubles into a box of Crayolas and pour them out in calming azure skies, warm yellow sunshine, radiant red flowers, and soothing green plants. In short, when I get down, I grab my crayons and color happy pictures and they cheer me way up.

Kelly B., Traveling Student
RFD, Montana

When I get one of those internal blowouts that sends me skidding off the happiness highway, I hit the real highway. I get in my car, roll down the windows, crank up some music—Pink Floyd usually—and drive the world away. Not too fast, not too slow. Just go with the flow. I don't care what the weather is—hot, freezing, muggy, wonderful, I don't care. I just want to dust the world off my shoulders.

**Tom R., Radio Programmer
Shreeveport, Louisiana**

I've got three blues chasers:

1. Cole Porter (original orchestrations, of course). The perfect word, the perfect rhyme, makes anything short of cancer fade into insignificance.

2. Setting a perfect table. Why be depressed when your guests will be devastated by your style and chic?

3. Libraries: one's own or others'. One's own is like seeing pieces of the past on a shelf. In a new, unexplored library, the thrill of discovering an unknown book takes one totally out of one's regular workaday world.

Tom M., Architectural Consultant
Norfolk, Virginia

When I get down, I call my sister at lunchtime when I know she's not home, disguise my voice, and leave a bizarre message on her answering machine. I pretend I'm Roseanne and accuse my sister of stealing my act. I threaten her with lawsuits and my ex-husband Tom Arnold. My sister can't figure it out! It always cheers me up. Of course, when she reads this, the cat's out of the bag and I won't be able to get away with it anymore. That's okay, I'm working on another impression that she'll never figure out.

Gladys M., Dog Groomer
Chicago, Illinois

I like to play hopscotch when I get the blues. There I am with my scotch in my right hand and hopping on my left foot. The trick is not to spill a drop. It doesn't work and that's over with . . . so are the blues.

Okay, one more. When I feel a low pressure center moving in, I stand on my head against a wall and drink nine sips of water through one of those crinkly straws like they give you in the hospital. I know what you're thinking—sounds more like a hiccup cure. Well, good thinking. It works for that too!

Raymond C., Retiree
West Melbourne, Florida

The blues? That's what they have down South, isn't it? Us Yankees don't have the blues. When we do, we go to Florida for the winter. But on the rare occasion when the dark side slips into my life, I mix up a favorite drink, put a tape on, relax in a soft chair, and listen to some good old polka music—guaranteed to get your heart pumping, your feet tapping, and put a smile on your face.

**Warren C., Legendary Amateur Baseball Player, Retired
Hadley, Massachusetts**

I have a simple formula to overcome the vicissitudes of daily life. I believe it would work for anyone else as well. When I'm alone and life is making me lonely, I go downtown. When I've got worries, all the noise and the hurry seems to help. You know, downtown. Things are great when I'm downtown. There's no finer place, I'm sure. Unless you live in Moonbeam, Arkansas, which I once did. Then you're S.O.L.

Bruce N., Restorer of Old Records
Citizen of the Universe (as we know it)

Natural
Wonders

I t's a world filled with mosquitoes, ticks, spiders and snakes. It's the Great Outdoors. There are creepy, crawly critters out there that go bump in the night and eat what they bump into to boot. But if you open your heart and mind to the great scheme of things, they are part of the beauty and grandeur of the world, and they don't really have a grudge against you; they just want a little bite!

In truth, it is a world of wonder open to the sun and stars. It is our destiny to live and share this world with all its creatures and all its natural beauty. Who is not happier when the sky is blue, the sun is shining, and the air is fresh. Spending time enjoying the natural wonders that surround even the most crowded city is a most natural habit to keep a happy heart.

When the blues come along, I get away from them. Wherever I'm living, I always have a special wild spot I go to. When I lived in Georgia, it was a pretty little lake not far from my house. I would take my dog—a beautiful mutt named Rollin'—and go there. We would walk the shore. As we did so, I would work to clear my mind of troubles and open it to the beauty and excitement of what was around me: the

foam of the little waves that lapped the shore, the debris they washed up, raccoon tracks in the mud, birds on the wing, leaves floating from the trees, the exuberance of my dog at running free in the wild.

Now I live in Nevada, and it is a special place in the desert I go to with my dog. We never fail to have a marvelous adventure. We find feathers from red-tailed hawks, beautifully colored stones, bones of long-gone elk and mule deer, wonderfully weathered manzanita branches, and we see wondrous critters that live in this silent land.

After one of these expeditions, I'm restored and ready to face whatever music is playing back in the real wild world.

**Janette M., Dancer
Las Vegas, Nevada**

Got the blues? Go to Alaska. Stay a month. Make sure it's a summer month. You can't be sad there. It's lovely country and it's light all the time. Not even seven flat tires in a day can get you down—slow you down, but not get you down.

Jordan S., Student
Kaysville, Utah

When I'm upset or need to think things over, I go horseback riding. There's something very peaceful and forceful about these animals. If the synergy is there, they can make you feel like a queen sitting astride a stallion. Of course, if it's not, you feel like a bothersome being who can easily be bucked off. If horses aren't available, it's a six-pack and a plate of brownies.

Lisa M., Artist Management
Nashville, Tennessee

My secret tip for happiness is to grow something. I don't care if it's a child, a puppy, a magnolia in the front yard, or a bean in a paper cup. Grow it. Growing something gives you a glimpse of harmony. Knowing harmony gives you a glimpse of peace. Knowing peace is beyond happiness.

Fred LaBour, Bassist
Joelton, Tennessee

think it's important to take a little time each day to
be with yourself. And, depending on the season,
that's how I stay centered.

In the winter, I take a little time each morning to
sit by my front window with a cup of coffee and watch
what goes on, in, around, and under a big magnolia
that grows on my front lawn. For example, when it
rains on magnolia leaves, it creates a steady drip-flow
from one big leaf to the one below and sounds like a
comforting, cozy little babbling brook.

In the spring, I sit on my front stoop with a cup of
hot tea at some point during each day and watch the
activity in the hedgerow that grows along my short
driveway—birds building nests, rustles in the under-
brush from little critters on early season missions of
their own, and, of course, the budding leaves and
flowers that emerge further and further with each
passing day.

Summers here are hot, so it is in the cool of the
evening that I take a few moments to sit on a lawn

chair with a cool beverage in my small backyard with my dogs. I especially like it just after the lawn has been mown. Smelling the grass, tasting the summer air, and I swear I can almost hear my garden growing.

Falls are wonderful. My favorite spot is a blanket under a crimson-colored maple tree that actually grows in my neighbor's yard but whose broad and leafy branches shelter part of mine as well.

**Pam M., Nurse
Practitioner
Nashville, Tennessee**

85

To keep a little space between myself and the blues, I go to a little pond near where I work and feed the ducks. I've done this so regularly that the ducks now know me by sight, and, as soon as they see me coming, they flock around and make one big happy quack after another . . . Quacks me up every time.

Joan J., Counselor
New Orleans, Louisiana

Happiness is to me not a subject of pursuit. I believe it is always around like sunlight and ready to enter our hearts. To make room for it, we need to find and remove the things that create selfish shadows in our souls.

Giving and forgiving are the two essential components of happiness.

Respect life. Be gentle. Speak easily with all creatures. Free flies and crawly creatures that wander inside your house.

Jerry G., Investment Coordinator
Bowling Green, Kentucky

Get outside. That's what I do. Nothing is drearier than four walls around me when I've got the worries, the willies, or the woe-is-me's. Just the act of getting outside and physically expanding my horizons puts me in a better frame of mind. If there's work to do outside, like leaf raking, weed pulling, or flower planting, I do that. Otherwise, I just wander around and take it all in. Even in a little yard like mine every nook and cranny is packed with nature, and there's always something to take in that takes a load off my mind.

Dot C., Family Counselor
Ottawa, Canada

The best cure for the blahs, blues, and blubbers I ever found is bare feet and warm green grass. Nothing's like wiggling your toes in good grass. You gotta smile. You gotta feel good. You gotta love it. Here's another idea. The Beach. Sand is as cool as grass . . . just don't smoke it. Let somebody else give a blues prescription for the cold months.

Freddy F., Jazz Musician
On the road

I gave happiness a lot of thought on a recent trip across the East Coast of America. It made for a very enjoyable drive over several days' time. I realized I have lots of happy habits—hugging trees, watching birds, smelling flowers, surrounding myself with people I love, planting seeds, smiling, deep breathing, relaxing in the shade, sleeping late on occasion, riding horses, playing tennis, and on and on.

Jean G., Herbalist
Woodstock, New York

I get the blues when it rains, and off I go into the rain. Why not? It's better to get drenched than to be a prisoner of precipitation, huddling in a confined space, fearing a little dampness. However, I do live in Florida, and while we seldom get a freezing rain, it is the lightning capital of the world. Instead of a leisurely walking along and singing in the rain, I am usually jumping in all directions to avoid those bolts. Still, there went those blues.

Harry C., Artist
South Florida

Who you live with has a lot to do with your happiness. We're fortunate in that we make each other happy.

Having said that, we believe that where you live also has a lot to do with happiness. We recently moved to a home on a wooded lot near a natural area and have discovered the truth in Shakespeare's words, "One touch of nature makes the whole world kin." The whole world in our case includes birds, butterflies, rabbits, chipmunks, squirrels, possums, foxes, turtles, and other crawling and flying creatures, even

an occasional deer. There is never a moment, summer or winter, when something alive is not moving outside our windows. We have come to not only recognize our fellow creatures but to know their families as well—to see them raise their own young and then bring them to our back door to take advantage of our permanent food bar.

Occasionally, a pair of eyes beams from the darkened woods, reminding us that we are the watched as well as the watchers.

What we have found in our woodland world is companionship that we did not know we had missed. We are sharing our lives with God's creatures, but we are also sharing experiences with each other that have kindled our spirits and sharpened our powers of observation. Together, we have regained a childhood sense of wonder that we may well have lost in the workaday world of adulthood. One touch of nature and we have been touched by nature.

**Ed and Janey G., Librarian-Archivist and Public Relations
Nashville, Tennessee**

The
Little
Bang
Theory

The Big Bang theory is how scientists think the universe began. Well, I'm not saying it didn't happen, but if it did, it only happened once. No phone numbers were exchanged. It was a cosmic one-night stand.

If you're waiting for a Big Bang to bring you happiness, you could be squandering a lifetime waiting for the dream of just one Big Moment. A person doesn't become happy in big gushes and explosions. Someone who feels good about life builds happiness one little moment at a time, one decision at a time, one smile at a time.

The full life, the happy life, comes from a sense of personal power, a belief that we can control, or at least influence, the internal and external forces that direct our lives.

Taking control over things we can and having an attitude of gratitude for the good things in our lives every day is the Little Bang Theory of Happiness.

Depression is a miasmic monster—a lurking, sneaking bastard emotion best approached as one might approach an arm-wrestling contest with King Kong. See it, recognize it, and run like hell. Run not from, but to something to counter the approaching shadow. Lights, noise, and people are good options; physical touch, if available from people and/or pets. Physical activity of any type, even vacuuming a floor.

These kinds of activities will keep the monster at bay, but to put it down and out I resort to inner resources. The beast feeds on self-pity, cannot survive without it, so one must adopt an "attitude of gratitude." I think of the people and critters I love and those who love me, ignoring those who do not. The next step for me is a conscious assessment of my immediate situation. My life at the moment.

Good health? Thank you, thank you.

Poor health? It could be worse. I recently endured nine weeks immobile and supine with a broken hip but without depression. How? My thoughts were directed to two dear friends, one of whom was living with an inoperable brain tumor, the other HIV positive, drifting daily towards the inescapable horror of AIDS. My bone was knitting. I would walk again.

Perspective is very important when dealing with depression.

But the most effective tool for me is reminiscence. I think about the good times, fun times, sweet times, and tender times with family, lovers, and friends. I fondle these memories like the treasures they are and hold them close. They warm me and some subtle magic from them dispels the dark, and in the clear light of reality I find myself content and often quite happy.

**Jay S., Executive Placement Consultant
Nashville, Tennessee**

think you have to take pleasure in the moment, in just living. If I open up my thoughts, I can always find something in what I'm doing to enjoy. I try to be conscious of the feel of the air I'm breathing, the colors around me, the texture of the things I touch. If the moment is so boring and unpleasant I can't find anything to enjoy about it, then I take satisfaction in the fact that I'm hanging in there and getting it done, that it's not beating me because I'm surviving it. That's worth a smile.

Of course, I have goals and dreams for the future and good and bad memories of the past, but those are places I visit. I can't sustain happiness by living in them. I live in the moment, and doing that keeps me happy.

Vernice A., Landscape Designer
Boulder, Colorado

I try to never want more than I can get. There's more to this than meets the eye. It doesn't mean that I don't have big ideas and goals and want things that are beyond my immediate reach. It means that I take things as they come, and if they don't come, they don't come. That's the key.

I went for the things that really make me happy a long time ago: a good wife and kids to come home to. If I've got that—and I do—the other things are just more gravy. Nice, but I don't really necessarily need them. Maybe if I had them I wouldn't even be happy with them. As my Aunt Carrie once told me, "You can only eat off one plate at a time."

John P., Sheetrock Hanger
Houston, Texas

My idea about staying happy is to have regular positive reinforcers coming at me all the time. That means positive people around me, an organized, comfortable place to live, the same for a place to work, and music that makes me feel good. This doesn't mean that I turn my back on friends who go through a bad period, but I won't sit around with them and listen to sad songs, and drink too much, and wallow in pain and misery. I insist they come into my world and be around my positive reinforcers.

**Daryll D., Laboratory Technician
St. Louis, Missouri**

The secret to being happy is not getting more, it's wanting less.

**Moses A., Guitar Player
A Holiday Inn Lounge Near You**

The moments are few and far between in my life when everything is really going right. I can't take all that time in between without a little joy. So I try to find moments of happiness in the everyday things that go on around me. The smell of fresh-cut grass, an old song I love on the radio, running on empty and just barely making it to the next gas station before I run out of gas, smiling and saying howdy to somebody I don't even know and having them smile and say howdy back at me. There are millions of little moments like these waiting for me everyday if I just open myself up to them. And I do. And they keep me fairly happy.

Michael G., Writer
Traveling in a mobile home

Your life is as good as you think it is. If you think your job sucks, it does. If you think your eggs are overcooked, they are. If you think I give a darn, I do, because I think my life is pretty good and I want yours to be good too.

Kathy M., Truck-stop Waitress
Houston, Texas

I spend some time thinking about the past and how things worked out then. Seems like for the most part, no matter how bleak they looked, somehow, some way, things worked out.

Hal P., Machinist
Elmville, Nebraska

f I can get out of bed in the morning, I stay happy all day. I just don't worry about things, and that includes the devil and his hurricanes. Let him do his damndest. I'm no youngster, I can't be cowed, and I won't live scared.

Bob D., Retiree
Key Largo, Florida

ou Maloney rhymes with UFO Baloney. That's what some wits (well, that's half right) have to say about me these days. Ever since I was abducted by aliens and given the power to see the future. But, I don't let them get me down, and nothing else does either. Because it happened. I can see tomorrow. And the future can always be happy if you know what's coming.

Lou M., Psychic
Sedona, Arizona

I haven't had a bad day since I learned to say no. I'm not talking about sex. I'm talking about being on this or that committee, in this or that club, a volunteer for this or that extracurricular duty. I even stopped renewing my magazine subscriptions. I went from a calendar with no uncommitted days on it, to one of national and personal holidays.

Judy N., Homemaker
Newark, New Jersey

I sat in the back of buses in the 1950s. I ate on the sidewalk because I couldn't sit down in a restaurant. I drank from a public water fountain marked "Colored Only." I cleaned other people's houses for a living and barely made a living.

Today, I ride where I want to on any bus. I eat in any restaurant I can afford. I drink water from any public fountain I choose. I'm too old to work, but I got Social Security and Medicare. I've got no reason, now, not to be happy except for the fact that I'm old.

Carrie W., Retiree
Dothan, Alabama

I stay happy by tuning in to the different rhythms of life. Every moment in life has its own rhythm. If you try to fight it, you get frustrated, like a dancer trying to force the beat of the music to match his steps instead of the other way around. Can't be done. You got to dance to the music that's being played. When I'm in the kitchen I find the rhythm of the work, groove with it, and everything goes along like a song. Fight that rhythm and food gets burned, plates get dropped, and one after another things go wrong. When I'm in my car during rush hour, I see people screaming and yelling because they can't go faster than the rhythm of the traffic will allow. Not me. I fit my groove to the flow around me. I watch the people, I check out their cars, I listen to the radio, I go when the light's green and stop when it's red. I don't try to beat it.

A. W. K., Cook
Atlanta, Georgia

When I was a small child,
   Happiness was a dry bed.
When I became an adult and fell in love,
Happiness was a shared bed.
Now that I am an old man,
Happiness is any bed.
This is the story of life.
Happiness depends on learning to
Appreciate fully whatever joy comes your way and to
Accept gracefully whatever else happens to you,
Because neither will last long
And, you can sleep afterwards.

Phil O., Retiree
RFD Kentucky

Enjoy being alone. But, also appreciate good friends and good conversation, especially over a table of thoughtfully prepared food and well-matched wine, graced silently to preserve the purity of the thankfulness.

Love your home, but travel well.

Be slow to anger, quick to forget; refuse to accept slights and insults.

Bar the pirates of Envy, Jealousy, and Resentment from your heart.

Do not fear death.

Always be polite. Courtesy is a mark of a secure person.

Return all telephone calls.

Remember all birthdays, but be thoughtful enough not to always mention them.

Be generous, but do not give simply to be thought good.

If you're unhappy without money, you won't be happy with it. Happiness is independent of wealth and fame. Happiness is a fullness of the heart, a humility and generosity that produces a serenity of the soul.

Jerry G., Business Consultant
Brentwood, Tennessee

I think happiness is having something to be enthusiastic about when you're not at work. Something totally unrelated to your job to get excited about.

For me, it's a 1948 Mercury I'm restoring. I've already restored a 1954 Pontiac for my wife. (I was born in 1948, and my wife, uh, just happens to like 1954 Pontiacs.) We cruise out every Saturday on a date in one of the two cars, and we always try to make it something special. Something to look forward to.

Fred B., Stonemason
Indianapolis, Indiana

Happiness for me is any time my brother is not practicing his cello.

Laurie Ann K., Third Grade Student
Ann Arbor, Michigan

I'm happy when I can go to the bathroom anytime I want to.

John B., Second Grade Student
Los Angeles, California

Every day I try to get a head start on tomorrow.

Bob M., Salesman
Seattle, Washington

There have been times when I've worked at jobs I didn't particularly enjoy or there were no flowers to smell or horses to ride. So, I can't always have what I want to be happy. This is where my most powerful habit helps out: looking for the good in all situations and giving thanks for this good. Doing this, for me, has created an endless flow of well-being and happiness in my life. It has now become such a habit that I don't really have to think about it anymore. The Good simply is and my Happiness simply is.

Jean G., Educator
Cullman, Alabama

There are 11 traffic lights between where I live and where I work. On a good day, I cruise through 7 or 8 of them. On a bad day, I'm stopped by all of them. During rush hour, which is when I'm talking about, the amount of my life that just one of these lights can cost me or save me is one minute and fifteen seconds. If I'm having a bad day and catch them all, that's a total of 13 minutes, 35 seconds they cost me. Now, in a 24-hour day, which is the only kind I can have, that's less than 1/96 of my time. But that 1/96 is critical, because it's what makes me on time for work or late for work. And more days than not, being on time for work is the difference between a good day and a bad day.

So, winning the daily battle of the traffic lights is how I stay mostly happy. Yes, it has cost me a lot of time with the calculator, driving the route, finding shortcuts around the block and through parking lots to get around the lights, but I have eliminated the commute to work as a thing that can cause me to have a bad day. This has made happiness possible for me. I recommend it for you, too. (Either that, or get up 13 minutes and 35 seconds earlier.)

Morris M., Computer Salesman
Atlanta, Georgia

I believe the world itself is not happy or unhappy. It's what you make it. I work at making it happy. I'm happy.

Dick M., Dentist
Washington, D.C.

firmly believe that if you're going to be happy you have to lose a few minutes out of every day. In other words, I slow down.

Instead of flying down the road, I go five miles under the speed limit. This takes away the double

stress caused by the fear of a traffic ticket as well as the fear of a serious accident.

Instead of running to grab the phone every time it rings, I let it ring until I get there by walking.

Instead of walking my dogs halfway around the block and pulling on their leashes every time they pause to sniff at something and commanding them to "Hurry up, I've got better things to do!" I walk them all the way around the block, and I take a little time to check out things myself—like the trees, the lawns, and the clouds.

Instead of telling my child not to bother me because I'm cooking supper, I put supper on hold for five minutes while he tells me about his day.

When my husband comes in the room, I take time to hug him—every time.

I guess what I'm saying is that I take time to be happy and that's my secret.

Mary B., Homemaker
San Diego, California

The blues usually stem from bad days. How I deal with this is by recognizing a bad day when I see it. You know a bad day when you see it. It starts out that way. Symptoms abound! When you wake up, the song you hate the most is playing on the clock radio. You forgot to put coffee and water in the coffeemaker the night before. You keep dropping the soap and you run

out of hot water. You're running late as you leave the house and your tank's on empty—talk about a metaphor—and the meeting you thought you had the morning to prepare for has been rescheduled to . . . the morning.

Plenty of warning. Plenty of time to adjust your attitude from "deal with it all" to just "getting through this day." On days like this, you have to take it as it comes, one little pain in the patoot at a time. Whatever happens, I just say to myself, "What do I need to do to get through this day? Tomorrow, I'll think about the rest of my life, today I just need to cope." That night, I don't try to cook dinner. I don't let my wife try to cook dinner. We go out, even if I have to charge it. Why risk burning down the house?

Sean R., Warehouse Manager
Trenton, New Jersey

When the big things in life start to get me down, I try to string together a series of cheap victories. Little jobs that need doing but are easy to put off, phone calls I've been needing to return, letters I've been needing to write, files that need organizing, an oil change for my car—just ordinary little things that need doing but are easily postponed. Doing a few of these gets my confidence up and I'm ready to tackle the big things again.

Felice A., Travel Agent
Orlando, Florida

You will think I'm weird and disgusting, but I'm not. Hear me out, don't just stop reading after this first sentence and you'll see I have a very good way to beat depression.

When I get blue, I think about cockroaches. They're disgusting and vile, but they've been around since the days of the dinosaurs. The dinosaurs are gone, but the cockroach lives on. When whatever happened happened, and dinosaurs couldn't find anything to eat, they got depressed, lost weight, and became extinct. Cockroaches, on the other hand, just found another way to keep on going, stayed alive, and stayed happy. Well, if a measly cockroach—the lowliest, most despised creature on this planet—can find a way to keep on going, stay alive, and stay happy, I can too!

John H., Attorney
Chicago, Illinois

Not writing other people's books for them makes me happy. I want to be paid if I do this. How's 50 cents a word sound?

Aaron N., Fourth Grade Student
Murfreesboro, Tennessee

Keeping a real grip on time is how I stay happy. Almost any job takes longer to do than you think it will. If I think I can do something in fifteen minutes, I plan for thirty. If I think a project can be done in two days, I plan on three. Building in a little extra time keeps my nerves from fraying. If I finish early, I use the time to get a head start on something else. I mean, if nothing else, there's always Christmas cards you can start addressing. Who will know you actually wished them a Merry Christmas in July?

Bonnie B., Claims Adjustor
Phoenix, Arizona

In t'ai chi, an ancient Chinese discipline involving meditative movements, one is taught to first figuratively, and then literally, "embrace the tiger." The tiger is anything that looms over you and because of fear, annoyance, indecision, or whatever, you avoid or run from it. By putting yourself in a frame of mind to embrace it—take it on—you remove it as a barrier to your happiness and growth.

Steve A., Writer
Austin, Texas

'm a strong person. I really try to learn from life. When things get really bad, I think to myself, "This will pass, and there most certainly is something to learn from it." It helps. It really does.

Other things that help keep me centered and bring me up from somewhere below the emotional equator to the happy latitudes are:

☛ Skinny dipping on a hot summer day. As I shed my clothes, I shed my daily cares. I enter the water; it is welcoming, soothing, refreshing, loving. I'm happy.

☛ Having a day with someone I really care about. My husband. It doesn't have to be anything unique and special; shopping, lunch, a movie, and preparing a nice dinner together at home is as special as it gets.

☛ A bubble bath at night with candles lit everywhere in the bathroom.

☛ Sitting on a quilt in a park or our backyard on a Saturday afternoon with a perfect glass of iced tea and "A Prairie Home Companion" on the radio.

☛ Crunchy shrimp sushi.

☛ Putting my toes in the ocean, then running from the water as the tide brings it in.

☛ Sitting very still and listening, with no sounds around but nature's. This is especially joyous after a hard day in the city.

☛ Memories of the red rocks of Sedona and the Grand Canyon the first time I saw them, and of the first kiss from the man I married—the kind of kiss you feel all the way down to your toes and that makes your knees weak.

Sally B., School Behavioral Consultant
Nashville, Tennessee

I stay happy by not putting things off. This is the greatest way there is to peace of mind.

Each day, I either deal with everything that comes up, or I schedule a day and time to deal with it. For example, when I bring in the mail, I go through it, pay the bills and answer any letters with a short note. In my leisure time, I write longer letters to friends and loved ones. I return phone calls as soon as possible, and I make the ones I dread first. I only dread that phone call for a short time, but I'm happy it's over with for a long time afterwards.

If I've got a problem with my wife, a relative, a friend, or a coworker, I look for a solution, and if I can't come up with one, I ask them to. I'm always willing to at least try a compromise. Keeping emotional roadblocks like these from blocking my path keeps me from feeling bogged down and helpless.

I try to never do more than one thing at a time. When I take a task on, I stay on it until it's done. There are no half-done chores around my house or office. It's surprising how much faster you can get things done by staying focused.

If this sounds terribly efficient, it is, but it's also easy to do. If you get a mind-set to act and not procrastinate, you find life is better, fuller, and there are more hours in the day. Plus, when I go to bed at night, I have accomplished things that day, and tomorrow is brighter because of it and this keeps me happy.

Edward A., Plumbing Contractor
Boise, Idaho

Happy Is As Happy Does

I learned as a little kid in school to "do unto others," and as I've grown, I've seen it's true that doing something for someone else helps get my mind off my own worries and warts.

Being around happy people is a great way to get happy ourselves. Happiness from a family member, friend, or coworker is contagious.

Sometimes happiness comes in a quiet, sneak-up-on-you kind of way. You make a little time to be with someone you love who could use your company or conversation. You don't do it to be happy; you do it because you love them and they want to be with you. Still, afterwards, you feel good about having done it and this gives you a nice little happy feeling. Try it with the family canine or feline—shoot out a big smile and a cheerful word and just see if Fido or Muffy doesn't send a grin right back! When you share moments with other people and critters you love, it comforts you both. Happy Is As Happy Does.

Someone once said to me, "Happiness is not knowing when you look around the room whether you're working or playing." I'm one of the few people in the universe who can honestly say I love, love, love, love, love what I do. I surround myself with wonderful people that help make my life full of accomplishments and they continue to teach me. 'Cause without learning and laughter, you can't be happy.

Mary M., Film/Music Video Producer
Nashville, Tennessee

My wife, my dogs, some good friends, some old honky-tonk rock 'n' roll 45s, a few pints of Boddington's best ale, that's all it takes for me . . . well, maybe some footage of Laurel and Hardy and Pele in their prime and a little extra vacation time and a stack of good books. Did I mention one of your books? No, I didn't think I did.

John P., Soccer Enthusiast and International Education Coordinator
Redwood City, California

When the grandkids are around, when they're not driving me crazy, they're good for lots of laughs. And when two-year-old Daniel comes over with his arms out saying, "Hug me," who could be sad?

Mary S., Homemaker
Washington, D.C.

My aunt Ginny always told me if I was feeling bad to stop focusing on myself and "get out there and do something for somebody." It's been good advice. If you make someone else smile, you will smile too. Instead of taking your blues out on someone, take them a smile. You may not get one back every time, but you'll never get a smile back if you give someone a scowl.

Kenneth L., Truck Farmer
Bangor, Maine

honestly believe that the best way to stay happy is to have an undemanding dog. Most of the time I can get a pretty fair share of understanding from my husband, and I can always count on a hug from my kids. But there are times when I need a friend who I know will love me no matter how crabby I get. And I can get crabby just as well as anybody else. My dog Al is the pal I turn to. Al is warm and fuzzy and, except for a little food and a trip outside every now and then, he never asks for anything. I curl up on the sofa; he lays beside me. I read; he softly snores. It's very comforting.

Maureen T., Computer Salesperson
San Francisco, California

We have four dogs (4)! One was chosen, the other three chose us. The only thing to be done with four dogs is to enjoy them. (Think about it, that's a lot of enjoyment.) I can sit and watch them for hours. They are all such great personalities and are so caught up in their own needs and desires that they provide a refreshing interlude to any day. They're happy pups and their happiness is contagious. It makes me happy too.

Catherine S., Business Executive
Kaysville, Utah

To beat back the blues, I take my sons on a picnic, eat watermelon, and watch them throw rocks in the water.

**Pat R., Electrician
Little Rock, Arkansas**

It makes me really happy to give gifts to people. It makes them smile. It makes me even happier if I can get them to laugh. Yep, that's what really makes me happy.

**Benjamin M., Middle School Student
Nashville, Tennessee**

How I escape the blues depends on what kind of blues I've got. Here are two of the ways I lose some of the blues.

☛ Pull out my child's baby book and look at all those adorable pictures of her as a baby. Such lovely memories come back to me. It's hard to be depressed when I remember how wonderful those moments were. (This may backfire on me when she's a teenager. Several of my friends have teenagers who think their parents are stupid right now. I'm afraid thinking about how sweet they were may depress someone living with a difficult adolescent.)

☛ Either be around optimistic uplifting people or be totally alone. Most of the time I can tell which of these options I need.

Jamie A., Television Producer
Fairview, Tennessee

When I feel a low coming on, I go out of my way to do something unexpected and nice for someone else. The look on their face always cheers me up.

Elizabeth D., Cab Driver
Boston, Massachusetts

After a hard day of putting up with my brother Aaron, I like to relax and play with Patches—my guinea pig—and my cat. Not at the same time. I also like to play tennis and write letters. If this one won't do I'll write you another one. Okay?

Marie N., Seventh Grade Student
Murfreesboro, Tennessee

My good health and happiness I credit to my family, my many friends, and especially my young friends. I love them for all the nice things they do to make my life happier.

Of course, that O. J. Trial and its aftermath have kept me pretty busy too.

Mrs. Connie M., Retiree
Nashville, Tennessee

I always have a pet, and I always make time each day to play with it. I have found this therapy works best if the pet has fur.

Candace G., Bookseller
Quebec, Canada

I stay happy by staying away from introversion. I extend myself, I take the first step. So many people are hesitant to step out and extend their hand. They are fearful of rejection. But that doesn't mean they're rejecting you. If you give them the chance, nine out of ten times they'll take your hand. That more than makes up for the one time they don't.

**David H., Martial Arts Instructor
Chicago, Illinois**

To be happy: I say pay attention to your family, put up lots of lights at Christmas time, coach baseball, and have yourself a pug dog for a friend.

Your family is your pride and joy. Nothing in your life takes more of you or gives more to you. Families are the most wonderful things in the world.

Christmas lights are a joy for everyone. The more the merrier.

Teach a kid how to hold a bat and how to be a good sport, not how to hit another kid or win at any cost, and you'll know why I love baseball.

A pug is always glad to see you and that can't help but cheer you up. When I'm not working, I take my pug, Beau, with me just about everywhere I go. Once, I pulled into a little market near where we live to pick up a gallon of milk. I left the motor running in my Toyota pickup and the air conditioner on for the dog.

It was summertime. Naturally, I also left the doors unlocked. Beau waited for me on the seat of the truck. As he saw me coming back with the milk, he got excited and jumped up against the driver's window. His paw accidentally pushed the lock down. I laughed. It was cute, a minor inconvenience. I headed around to the passenger side. He saw me going there. He went there too. He jumped up on the window and locked the other door too. I'm locked out in the heat, the pug is locked in the air conditioned truck cab with the motor running, looking at me like I'm an idiot because I'm laughing like one. So did my wife when I called her to bring a spare key, so does everyone else I tell this story to. You gotta love a dog that can make everyone laugh.

Jimmy O., Court Reporter
Knoxville, Tennessee

If you want to be happy, you have to make happiness. Just like if you want to have money you have to make it. I try to make a little happiness everywhere I go. I smile, I say "Howdy!" and I go out of my way to do at least one unasked-for favor for somebody every day of my life.

Bruce B., Woodworker
St. Paul, Minnesota

Happiness to me is a pot filled with glitter. It's been that way ever since I was a little baby girl sitting on my mama's knee. On my birthday and other special occasions, she would give me little packages of glitter, each a different color. I would mix them all up in the same pot and have oodles of multicolored glitter. Then when people came in the door, I'd toss glitter at them and yell, "Fairy dust!"

To this day, glitter is a big part of my happiness. I put it in birthday and Christmas cards. I even toss it on my husband every now and then when he's been cranky. (This works better on my kids). I keep a big pot of it and I'm always dipping into it. Spreading glitter spreads happiness.

Louise G., Tax Consultant
Franklin, Kentucky

My two little secrets are simple:

1) Every morning I count my blessings before I get out of bed—unless one of my little blessings is crying, and then I get out of bed, cradle her in my arms and count my blessings while I walk her around the house.

2) Realizing that energy is energy, energy spent in remorse, regret, negativity, spite, anger, etc., *can* be redirected and expressed as joy, creativity, gratitude, forgiveness, used toward work or play or in good deeds, volunteerism or charity or the like.

Douglas G., Musician
Nashville, Tennessee

When I'm in a mood of feeling sorry for myself, I often see myself sinking into a trench. I know I have to get out! So I put on my Mary Englebreit baseball cap that says "Knock it off!" and walk around my neighborhood trying to think of somebody who's probably worse off than me. I stop at a neighbor's and knock on the door. If they let me in, I start the conversation by saying something like, "You've been on my mind and I was just wondering how you're doing." Well, there are very few people who won't take that kind of an invitation to start spilling their guts about the little things (or big things) that are bothering them. I don't even have to talk—I just listen and throw in a few words of encouragement. After a while, I go home feeling *much* better about my own problems and knowing that somebody else probably feels a little lighter for having dumped their troubles on me.

Maggie S., Editor
Ogden, Utah

Epilogue

Some people see life as a game. If that's true, then life as a human being is without a doubt the Mother of Major Leagues. You are in the big time, just by being alive. But, unlike baseball, if you mess up, play poorly, and trip over your own feet, they still can't send you back to the minors. You are big league no matter what anybody else has to say about it. So, step up to the plate and take a big swing. Whether you get a hit or not, keep on swinging! You're a Big Leaguer and that's your job!